Dedication

To my family – thank you for your enduring belief and support. I love you always – Mom, Dad, Tate & Owen.

To those with a chip on their shoulder & a spark in their heart – keep going.

Acknowledgments

GENERAL PARTNERS

Cokie Hasiotis
David Hoang
Lorenzo De Boni
Anthony Goonetilleke
Wisam Abdulla
Zach Waterfield

Rebeccah Wrady
Lonnie Hill
Myles Cheatum
Mariano Gonzalez
Eric Bahn
Marlon Stevenson
Aadil Maan

Ali Finkelstein
Keiver Tremblay
Justin Potts
Vinay Patankar
Alexander B Bates
Salahuddin Sirajuddin

PRINCIPALS

Hunter Owens
Leann Abad
John Thomey
Abena Anim-Somuah
Robyn Weller

Logan Breslin
Tara Doherty
Gefen Skolnick
Fabiola Cazares
Kat Cole

Sandy Kwon
Jamie Melzer
Michael Young
Milos Milosevic
Turner Novak

ASSOCIATES

Shreya Sudarshana
Scott Orn
Gaby Goldberg
Abdul Ajetunmobi
Sid Jha
Parker Henderson
DC Cassidy

Shenita Gao
Stephanie Manning
Neel Somani
Ellen DaSilva
Christopher Joseph
Drew Volpe
Nawaz Ahmed
Elizabeth Yin

Adam Towers
Mads Jensen
Patrick Matthews
Chase Dun
Ian Dilick
Ursula Rossi Becker
Macy Fox

ANALYSTS

Halle Kaplan-Allen
David Wong
Doug Rixmann
Cat Kricorian
Jose Eduardo Ruano

Rachel Masterson
Michael Smith
Dana Iverson
Wilson Galyean
Tyler Bradshaw

Ashwin Jadhav
Mathew Sherman
Suraya Shivji
Grace Myers
Greg Montemurro

Foreword By Ann Miura-Ko

Throughout my career, I've had incredible people with enormously successful careers give me a chance, provide guidance, or a word of encouragement just when I needed it. I believe that this magic has been the secret to my journey as a venture capitalist juggling parenting three kids, partnering with a CEO spouse, caretaking aging parents, and teaching at Stanford.

Today, when I look around, there are massive problems in our society and world that need to be addressed. Some days it feels overwhelming. But, I also get to meet entrepreneurs, go getters, dreamers, visionaries who are often young and on the precipice of greatness. Today, these people share all of the knowledge they gain to help accelerate the world around them in newsletters, blogs, tweets and even TikToks. I think this is what gives me eternal optimism.

Paige is a great example of this for me. She's not only created her own investing practice through sheer willpower and hard work, she is also sharing all of her knowledge with those around her so that these opportunities are becoming more democratized.

My hope is that inspiring young underrepresented investors to get into the game and demystifying the process so that it doesn't seem like an out of reach opportunity will enable more voices around the table to advocate for entrepreneurs in all reaches of the world.

Before we begin, a bit of background on venture capital: Venture capital (VC) is a special type of investing that focuses specifically on "risky" investments in potential high-growth startups.

It has been crucial to the beginnings and growth of many now household names - Apple, Google, Facebook, and more.

Venture capitalists (VCs) are the people who invest in these companies & through this book, together we will demystify what they do, why they are important, and how they make decisions.

I hope you all enjoy!

– Paige Finn Doherty

@paigefinnn

Before starting a farm, you should have a good idea of what you want to grow.

And just like a farmer decides what they want to grow, a venture capitalist decides what they want to invest in.

An **investment thesis** helps a venture capitalist make decisions on what companies to invest in and help grow. It commonly includes stage and sector.

At its core, an investment thesis is your unique view on what you can help become most fruitful in the future.

Before a farmer starts a farm, they'll often try gardening on a smaller scale.

Similarly, a venture capitalist will often start by investing on a smaller scale with their personal capital (angel investing) or organizing syndicate deals.

When a farmer has shown promise growing a smaller number of crops, they'll look to their network to raise money for a farm.

Similarly, when an investor has shown promise growing companies from angel investing, they'll look to their network to raise money for a fund. This process is called fundraising.

These investors will put together a pitch deck, a presentation consisting of:

- their investment thesis
- their past performance investing
- their professional background
- their fund structure

After putting together their pitch deck, a venture capitalist will start on the road to fundraising. The average time to raise a first fund is between 12 and 16 months.

The people who agree to commit money to a venture capital fund are called limited partners, or LPs.

After gathering commitments of money, a farmer needs to find seeds to grow crops. Similarly, after their funding, a venture capitalist needs to find companies to invest in. There are two ways to do this: inbound and outbound sourcing.

Inbound sourcing happens when investors, founders, or Twitter followers send companies toward a VC.

Outbound sourcing happens when venture capitalists reach out to founders about their companies.

HEY! We should buy carrots.

When a farmer finds seeds they think might be a good fit for their farm, they evaluate them. Similarly, when a venture capitalist finds companies they think might fit their fund, they evaluate them.

Here are three of the common lenses they evaluate companies through:

product-
market fit

founder-
industry fit

fund fit

Let's talk about product-market fit first. Just like a farmer would evaluate a seed for its ability to grow in a certain climate, a venture capitalist would evaluate a company's ability to grow in a certain market.

How will this seed grow in this climate?

How will this seed grow in this market?

What special characteristics will make it grow better here?

What special characteristics will make this company grow better than its competitors?

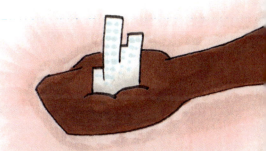

Let's talk about founder-industry fit. Just as a farmer will evaluate a certain seed on its past growing, a venture capitalist will evaluate a company based on its founder and team's previous experience in the company's industry.

How have this seed's crops grown in the past?

How has this team grown successfully together in the past?

Let's talk about fund fit. Just as a farmer who grows corn will want to grow more corn, a venture capitalist with a specific investment thesis will want to invest in companies within their investment thesis.

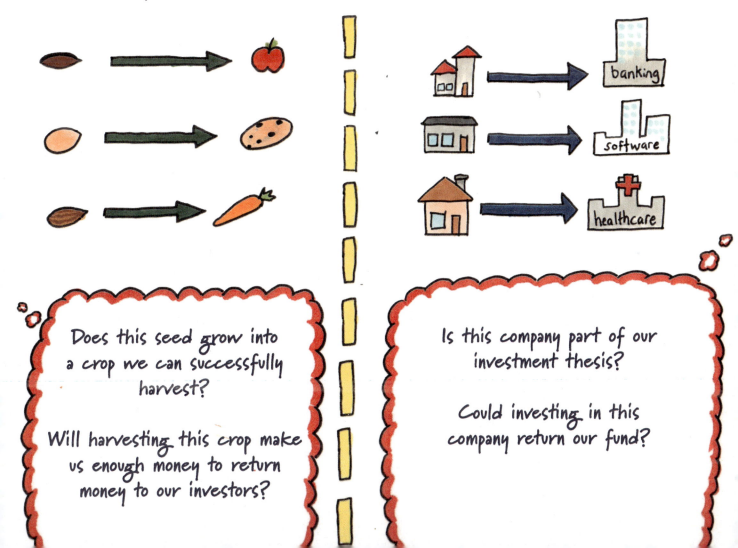

Does this seed grow into a crop we can successfully harvest?

Will harvesting this crop make us enough money to return money to our investors?

Is this company part of our investment thesis?

Could investing in this company return our fund?

There's another aspect—timing. Just like a seed may check all the boxes for a farmer in fall, but it needs to be planted in summer, a company may check all the boxes for a venture capitalist, but the timing isn't right.

There is a season for everything—
sometimes it's not this one. Farmers
and venture capitalists learn that
patience is crucial.

Based on the evaluation done through these lenses, a venture capitalist will either pass on a company or offer a term sheet.

A term sheet is a non-legally binding document provided by a venture capitalist to a company's founder. It outlines the terms of a potential investment agreement.

After specific terms are negotiated, the venture capitalist will proceed with due diligence, a deeper dive into the company they will potentially invest in.

They'll ask past and current customers about their experiences with the company. These are called customer reference calls.

They'll take a closer look at the actual finances of the business.

They'll spend time thinking about potential risks, and how this founder and company are best positioned to overcome them.

This due diligence process lasts anywhere from a few weeks to a few months.

How was your experience?

After going through a rigorous due diligence process, a venture capitalist will prepare an investment memo that covers their investment recommendation, the terms from the term sheet, and their findings from the due diligence process.

Founder

Pitch

venture capitalist

investment memo

Limited partner

Because venture capitalists don't often keep the money for their fund in the bank, they will then perform a capital call, telling their LPs to send them the money for the investment.

Founder

Money

Equity

venture capitalist

Limited partners

Limited partners

Just like a farmer's responsibility is to help their seeds grow after purchasing them, it is a venture capitalist's responsibility to help the companies they've invested in (now called their portfolio companies) grow.

Each crop is different, just like each company is, so some will need more care and attention than others.

Just like farmers store extra grain in silos for future seasons, some venture capitalists save up to half of their initial funds for future funding rounds in their fastest growing companies.

This "extra store" is often called follow-on funding.

While a farmer is mainly responsible for helping plants grow, they're also responsible for running their farm—making sure the equipment is tuned up, building relationships with their investors, and handling the day-to-day aspects of the business, like finances.

Similarly, while a venture capitalist is mainly responsible for sourcing and helping their portfolio companies grow, they also have to tend to their investors (referred to as investor relations) and run the fund as a business (referred to as fund operations).

A farmer can manage a smaller farm by themselves, but once they start caring for lots of crops, things can get overwhelming. Similar to how farmers hire farm hands, venture capitalists hire teams to help them invest in lots of different companies.

Here's an idea of what these teams look like:

general partners

principal

vice presidents

associates & analysts

At the end of every growing season comes a harvest. This is true in farming and also venture capital.

In venture capital, harvesting is referred to as "exiting" companies. Just like farmers get a slice of the profits from their harvest, venture capitalists get a slice of the profits from their exits, called carried interest, or "carry." There are a handful of different ways to exit:

get acquired

go public

There are two types of waterfalls for carry: the American waterfall, which applies on a deal-by-deal basis, and the European waterfall, which applies on an integrated or fund-level basis.

One VC firm is constantly in this cycle—

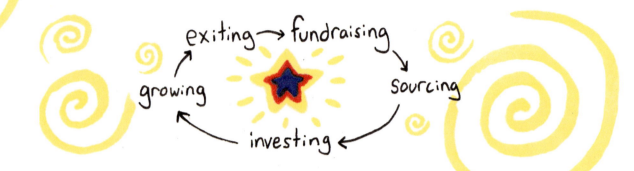

exiting → fundraising

growing

sourcing

investing

—and they often raise another fund two or three years after their initial raise. A fund life cycle, from raising to the last portfolio company exit, is usually ten years.

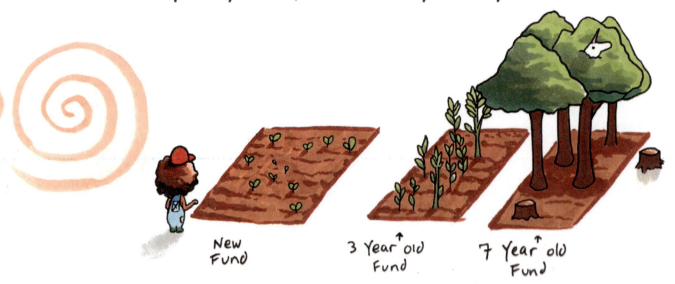

New Fund

3 Year old Fund

7 Year old Fund

One of the most important responsibilities of a venture capitalist is to train and nurture other aspiring venture capitalists, teaching them how to invest in and help grow companies that shape the world around us. That might just be you one day.

It's incredible to imagine all this started from just a seed—an idea of what might be fruitful in the future.

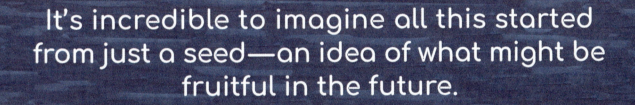

Much like farmers, venture capitalists play a relatively hidden role in shaping the world we know today.

That influence is why diversity in investors is so important. By including a wide range of views we can shape a world that reflects the dynamic nature of our population.

Made in the USA
Las Vegas, NV
27 October 2022

58275361R00026

PAIGE FINN DOHERTY
ILLUSTRATED BY OWEN DOHERTY
Copyright © 2021 Paige Finn Doherty
All rights reserved.
ISBN: 978-0-578-90645-4